GREAT MOMENTS IN
WORLD CUP HISTORY

Diane Bailey

WORLD SOCCER BOOKS™

rosen publishing's
rosen central®
New York

Published in 2010 by The Rosen Publishing Group, Inc.
29 East 21st Street, New York, NY 10010

Library of Congress Cataloging-in-Publication Data

Bailey, Diane, 1966–
Great moments in World Cup history / Diane Bailey.—1st ed.
    p. cm.—(World soccer books)
Includes bibliographical references and index.
ISBN 978-1-4358-9139-5 (library binding)
ISBN 978-1-61532-875-8 (pbk)
ISBN 978-1-61532-876-5 (6 pack)
1. World Cup (Soccer)—History—Juvenile literature. I. Title.
GV943.49.B33 2010
796.334—dc22

2009020046

Manufactured in China

CPSIA Compliance Information: Batch #HW10YA: For Further Information contact Rosen Publishing, New York, New York at 1-800-237-9932

On the cover: Top: Surrounded by his teammates, Italy's Fabio Cannavaro lifts the World Cup trophy in triumph after Italy beat France in 2006. Bottom: Bobby Moore, the captain of England's 1966 squad, embraces the Jules Rimet trophy to celebrate a win over Germany.

CONTENTS

INTRODUCTION

Soccer caused problems. That was the conclusion of storekeepers in medieval London, England. All that roughhousing! Balls flying everywhere! Customers were not safe in the streets. The merchants appealed to the king. He agreed to help out. He outlawed soccer in the city. Years later, other kings tried to discourage soccer. They decided it was distracting to young men, who were supposed to be practicing how to throw javelins.

These early attempts to snuff out soccer did not work. It is now the most popular sport in the world. There are teams on every continent—even Antarctica. It unites people of every race and color. There is no language barrier to the cheer that goes up when the ball hits the net.

Soccer's best players and national teams meet at the World Cup, a global competition. The first World Cup was held in 1930, but its beginnings were more than 25 years earlier. In 1904, a French journalist named Robert Guérin invited representatives from several different countries to discuss the idea of forming an international soccer organization. People from Belgium, France, Holland, Spain, Sweden, Switzerland, and Denmark met in Paris. They formed the Fédération Internationale de Football Association (FIFA).

The young organization struggled. In 1906, FIFA tried to organize an international tournament. It is sometimes called "the first World Cup." But the event flopped. Then World War I started. The war made communication and travel too difficult for an event that would involve several countries. However, soccer was being played at the Olympics. FIFA's third president, Rimet, was inspired by this success. He decided to give the World Cup idea another try. In 1928, FIFA decided that the tournament would be held every four years. The first one would be held in 1930. Jules Rimet went to work rounding up competitors. An artist designed a trophy. In 1930, only 13 countries participated. By 1954, the number of countries had risen to 16. For the qualifying rounds of 2010, a record 204 countries competed for one of 32 spots!

Rimet's dream was to spread soccer all over the world. Now FIFA has more members than the United Nations or the Olympic committee. Soccer is the most international sport there is. Every four years, it is watched by the whole world.

When one World Cup ends, preparation for the next begins. Today, the national soccer (or football) team of a country spends years training and planning strategy. It wasn't like that in 1930, the year the first World Cup was held. Then some countries couldn't even decide whether to go or not.

THE FIRST WORLD CUP

In 1929, the Fédération Internationale de Football Association (FIFA) decided that Uruguay would host the first tournament. Uruguay had won the Olympic title in soccer in 1928. FIFA decided the country deserved the honor.

Two months before the event, however, no European countries had signed up to play. The ship voyage from Europe to Latin America took three weeks. Plus, it was expensive. No one wanted to go.

But Jules Rimet was determined. He talked Belgium, France, Romania, and Yugoslavia into coming from Europe. Eight more teams came from Latin America. The United States also sent a team. In total, only 13 teams played.

On July 13, 1930, a piece of World Cup history was made. During the playoff rounds, France played Mexico. France won, but that was not the important part. The moment to remember was when Lucien Laurent scored France's first goal. In most ways, it was just a regular goal, not especially tricky

WORLD CUP URUGUAY 1930

WINNER
URUGUAY

FINAL STADIUM/CITY
CENTENARIO/MONTEVIDEO

FINAL SCORE
URUGUAY 4, ARGENTINA 2

GOLDEN SHOE WINNER
GUILLERMO STÁBILE,
ARGENTINA (8)

PARTICIPANTS
13

MATCHES
18

NUMBER OF GOALS/AVERAGE
70/3.9

NUMBER OF SPECTATORS/AVERAGE
434,500 / 24,138

A Uruguayan player makes the team's first goal in the finals against Argentina in 1930. Uruguay won, 4–2, and became the first World Cup winner.

or skillful. But it was very special in one way. It could not be repeated, ever again. Laurent had scored the World Cup's very first goal.

France lost to Argentina in the next round. In this match, the referee accidentally ended the match six minutes too soon. Many people pointed out his mistake. He agreed to restart the game.

During that first World Cup, everyone was still learning how to do things. For the final between Uruguay and Argentina, the teams couldn't decide what ball to use. In the end, they compromised: they used Argentina's ball for the first half, and Uruguay's for the second.

Uruguay got the first goal. Then Argentina scored twice. In the second half, Uruguay scored twice more. They took the lead back, and then scored once more. Uruguay was the first World Cup winner.

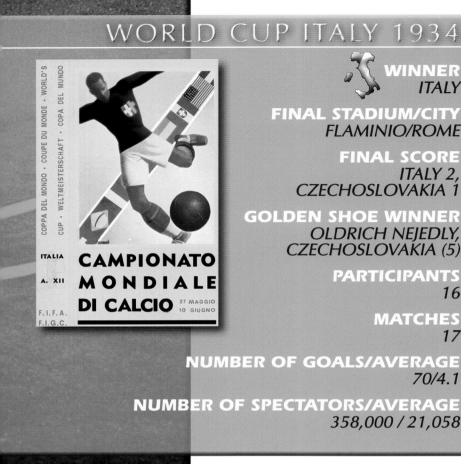

WORLD CUP ITALY 1934

CAMPIONATO MONDIALE DI CALCIO

WINNER
ITALY

FINAL STADIUM/CITY
FLAMINIO/ROME

FINAL SCORE
ITALY 2,
CZECHOSLOVAKIA 1

GOLDEN SHOE WINNER
OLDRICH NEJEDLY,
CZECHOSLOVAKIA (5)

PARTICIPANTS
16

MATCHES
17

NUMBER OF GOALS/AVERAGE
70/4.1

NUMBER OF SPECTATORS/AVERAGE
358,000 / 21,058

IN THE SHADOW OF POLITICS

The next World Cup was held in 1934 in Italy. Italy was ruled by dictator Benito Mussolini at the time. Mussolini was a Fascist. A Fascist requires people to submit to the government's ideas. Mussolini did not even care about soccer. But he did like the idea of Italy, and himself, being in the spotlight.

This time there was no shortage of interest in playing. Thirty-two teams would compete for 16 final slots. One team missing was Uruguay. They were upset that Italy had refused to come to Uruguay in 1930. So they refused to go to Italy. It's the only time in the history of the World Cup that the reigning champions have not returned to defend their title.

The Italian soccer players were under a lot of pressure. Mussolini made it clear that Italy should win. Thanks in large part to Giuseppe Meazza, they did. Meazza had learned to play soccer as a boy on the streets of Milan. He later became soccer's first international star. He was an excellent dribbler and shooter, and he helped Italy move up through the rounds. However, the winning goal, against Czechoslovakia, was a fluke by Italian player Raimondo Orsi. He later tried to demonstrate the shot, but he could never do it again.

With proud fans looking on from the stands, the Italian players lift their coach, Vittorio Pozzo, as they celebrate their 1934 World Cup victory over Czechoslovakia.

WIN OR DIE

Four years later, in 1938, France was the host. France was Jules Rimet's home country. He hoped to increase soccer's popularity there.

Politics again influenced the World Cup. Adolf Hitler was the leader of Germany. He was a soccer fan and made sure the 1938 German team had world-class players. Some of them came from Austria. As World War II loomed, Germany had taken over Austria. Hitler took the best Austrian soccer players and made them play for Germany.

The Italians were still under pressure from Mussolini. He sent a telegram to the team that said, "Win or die."

Giuseppe Meazza had been the star of Italy's 1934 team. In 1938, he was caught with his pants down—literally! He ripped his pants early in the game, and later they fell down. His team-mates had to make a circle around him until new pants were delivered.

Italy won the final match against Hungary to defend its title. After the game, the Hungarian goalkeeper showed no regrets. He had heard about Mussolini's threatening telegram. He said, "I may have let in four goals, but at least I saved their lives." Later, how-ever, people pointed out that the telegram's message might not have been as dire as it seemed. To the Italians, "Win or die" could have been just an extreme way of saying, "Do your best." Only Mussolini knew whether his message was a true threat or just enthusiastic encouragement.

WORLD CUP FRANCE 1938

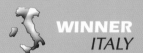

WINNER
ITALY

FINAL STADIUM/CITY
STADE COLOMBES/PARIS

FINAL SCORE
ITALY 4, HUNGARY 2

GOLDEN SHOE WINNER
LEONIDAS, BRAZIL (7)

PARTICIPANTS
15

MATCHES
18

NUMBER OF GOALS/ AVERAGE
84/4.7

NUMBER OF SPECTATORS/AVERAGE
376,000 / 20,888

BACK TO THE GAME

The 1938 World Cup was the last for more than a decade. In 1942, what would have been World Cup IV was overshadowed by World War II. Most of Europe, as well as the United States, were heavily involved in the war. The 1942 and 1946 tourna-ments were canceled. The World Cup trophy stayed in a shoebox under the bed of a FIFA official.

It would be 1950 before the World Cup was played again. This time it was in Brazil. Brazil built a

Giuseppe Meazza (left), the captain and star of Italy's team, shakes hands with Hungarian captain Gyorgy Sarosi before the two teams battle for the 1938 title.

WORLD CUP BRAZIL 1950

WINNER
URUGUAY

FINAL STADIUM/CITY
MARACANÃ/RIO DE JANEIRO

FINAL SCORE
URUGUAY 2, BRAZIL 1

GOLDEN SHOE WINNER
ADEMIR MENEZES, BRAZIL (9)

PARTICIPANTS
13

MATCHES
22

**NUMBER OF GOALS/
AVERAGE**
88/4.0

NUMBER OF SPECTATORS/AVERAGE
1,043,500 / 47,431

brand-new stadium called the Maracanã. It was so big that the radio announcers, who sat high in the stadium, could not see the players on the ground very well. So in 1950, the players wore numbers on their jerseys for the first time.

Thirteen countries participated. England was playing in its very first World Cup. They had an excellent team. The United States, on the other hand, had one of the worst teams. The U.S. players didn't even play soccer full-time. One of their players was Joe Gaetjens. He had been washing dishes in a restaurant only a month earlier.

The United States played England in an early round. The outcome was considered obvious: England would win. The U.S. players were enthusiastic, but England was better. The game had only one goal. That was enough of a surprise, but the real shocker was who scored it—a former dishwasher. The United States had beaten England! This is still remembered as one of the biggest upsets in soccer history.

Host Brazil also had a strong team. The *verde amarela* had an easy first round, scoring seven goals in their three games against Mexico, Switzerland, and Yugoslavia. Later, Brazil destroyed the Swedish defense with a 7–1 result in the second round, and repeated the performance against Spain with a final result of 6–1. Brazilian striker Ademir scored eight goals in the cup, including a hat trick (three goals in one game) against Sweden. Everyone thought they would win, including Uruguay, who played them in the finals. It

Stunned Brazilian fans watch Uruguay's Ghiggia score against Brazil during the 1950 World Cup final. Brazil, the heavy favorite to take the title, endured the "Maracanã tragedy" when they lost 2–1 to Uruguay.

was Uruguay's first time back at the tournament since 1930. More than 200,000 people filled the Maracanã for the final. Brazil had played well in the early rounds. In fact, they didn't even have to win the game in order to win the World Cup. They only had to tie. The first half was scoreless, but in the second half Brazil made the first goal. Brazil's fans thought the win was secured. Then Uruguay tied the score. Could Brazil hold off Uruguay for a few more minutes?

They couldn't. Uruguay scored again. It was too late for Brazil to rally. The stunned Brazilian fans couldn't believe it. Their team had been bested, in their home country, in their new stadium. They called it the Maracanã tragedy.

Despite this loss, Brazil still had much more to say on the subject of soccer. They would do so later that decade.

CHAPTER 2

THE WORLD'S GAME

In 1954, FIFA turned 50. Soccer's popularity was spreading throughout the world. Most of the interest was still in Europe and Latin America, but other countries were catching on. Africa and Asia began to field teams. South Korea and Turkey competed in 1954. Four years later, Northern Ireland, Wales, and the Soviet Union played. Bulgaria entered in 1962, and Portugal and North Korea joined in 1966.

The United States was a notable exception. The Americans were brawny and cheerful, but their win over England in 1950 had been a fluke. No one thought they actually matched England's skill. However, the win made headlines—and headlines can sometimes start a movement. In this case, though, the United States did not build on its victory.

An important addition to soccer in the 1950s had nothing to do with the game or the players. In 1954, for the first time, soccer came to the fans— thanks to a new device called television.

WORLD CUP SWITZERLAND 1954

WINNER
WEST GERMANY

FINAL STADIUM/CITY
WANKDORF/BERNE

FINAL SCORE
W. GERMANY 3, HUNGARY 2

GOLDEN SHOE WINNER
SANDOR KOCSIS,
HUNGARY, 11

PARTICIPANTS
16

MATCHES
26

NUMBER OF GOALS/AVERAGE
140/5.4

NUMBER OF SPECTATORS/AVERAGE
889,500 / 34,211

BATTLES AND MIRACLES

Hungary came to the 1954 World Cup in Switzerland feeling confident—and rightly so. Their national team had been undefeated for 31 games over a stretch of 4 years. Hungary's "Magical

Gyula Grosics, Hungary's goalkeeper, goes airborne to stop a shot from a West German player. Behind by two goals, West Germany rallied for an unexpected 3–2 win against Hungary, which had been undefeated for years.

Magyars" seemed to possess not just skill and luck but perhaps a little bit of magic.

The star of the Hungarian team was Ferenc Puskás. He was an inside forward with a powerful left foot. If Hungary was going to bring home a trophy, Puskás would certainly be part of it.

The coach of the West German team noticed something in the schedule. Even if West Germany lost to powerful Hungary, they could still advance in the tournament. In the match, the West German coach played second-string players and got trounced by Hungary. However, the team's starting lineup was fresh. Also, during this first match, Hungary's Puskás had hurt his ankle. The injury bothered him for the rest of the tournament.

Hungary met Brazil in the quarterfinals. Hungary won, but it was an unusually rough match. After the game, a fight broke out in the locker room. The Hungarians and Brazilians had it out until the Swiss police came to break things up. This was called the "Battle of Berne," but Hungary still had more battles to fight.

They won again in the semifinals against Uruguay, but they played hard for it. The Hungarian team was getting tired. West Germany, on the other hand, got an easy win over Austria.

The finals pitted Hungary against West Germany. Puskás was injured but still played valiantly. He scored Hungary's first goal. Hungary scored again before West Germany surged ahead with three

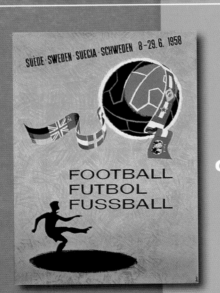

WORLD CUP SWEDEN 1958

SUÈDE · SWEDEN · SUECIA · SCHWEDEN 8-29.6. 1958

FOOTBALL
FUTBOL
FUSSBALL

WINNER
BRAZIL

FINAL STADIUM/CITY
RASUNDA/STOCKHOLM

FINAL SCORE
BRAZIL 5, SWEDEN 2

GOLDEN SHOE WINNER
*JUST FONTAINE,
FRANCE (13)*

PARTICIPANTS
16

MATCHES
35

NUMBER OF GOALS/AVERAGE
126/3.6

NUMBER OF SPECTATORS/AVERAGE
909,580/26,273

Overcome with emotion, Brazilian legend Pelé (center) clings to goalkeeper Gylmar Dos Santos Neves in 1958. Pelé helped his team take a 5–2 win over Sweden at his World Cup debut.

goals. Puskás made a heroic last attempt and kicked the ball into the net. However, the referee ruled that he was not in the correct position. The goal didn't count. West Germany called the win the "Miracle of Berne." They had ended the magic for Hungary.

NEW STANDARDS

The 1958 World Cup in Sweden brought new approaches. Brazil brought a nutritionist and a psychologist. Sweden hired cheerleaders. As for the actual soccer, it set new standards, too.

The tournament was notable for not only one but two events. The first came at the hands of French player Just Fontaine. Fontaine was not even on France's starting lineup. He replaced an injured player. Certainly no one could have ever expected his amazing performance on the field. Fontaine, playing in six matches, scored a whopping 13 goals throughout the tournament. More than 50 years later, that record still stands as the most goals ever scored in a single World Cup.

The other surprise came from Brazil. The talent on Brazil's team ran deep. The field veterans had a suggestion for their coach. Why didn't he use

WORLD CUP CHILE 1962

WINNER
BRAZIL

FINAL STADIUM/CITY
NACIONAL/SANTIAGO

FINAL SCORE
BRAZIL 3,
CZECHOSLOVAKIA 1

GOLDEN SHOE WINNER
GARRINCHA, BRAZIL (4)
VALENTINE IVANOV,
SOVIET UNION (4)
LEONEL SANCHEZ, CHILE (4)
FLORIAN ALBERT,
HUNGARY (4)
DRAZEN JERKOVIC,
YUGOSLAVIA (4)
VAVA, BRAZIL (4)

PARTICIPANTS
16

MATCHES
32

NUMBER OF GOALS/AVERAGE
89/2.8

NUMBER OF SPECTATORS/AVERAGE
899,074 / 28,096

Czech goalkeeper Viliam Schrojf and Brazilian player Vava leave the ground behind as they battle for control of the ball. Their teammates stand ready for action during

WORLD CUP ENGLAND 1966

WINNER
ENGLAND

FINAL STADIUM/CITY
WEMBLEY/LONDON

FINAL SCORE
ENGLAND 4, W. GERMANY 2

GOLDEN SHOE WINNER
EUSÉBIO, PORTUGAL (9)

PARTICIPANTS
16

MATCHES
32

NUMBER OF GOALS/AVERAGE
89/2.8

NUMBER OF SPECTATORS/AVERAGE
1,635,000 / 51,093

some of the younger players on the bench?

The coach agreed. For the next match against the Soviet Union, he sent in Garrincha (the nickname for Manuel Francisco dos Santos), a 24-year-old who had overcome polio as a child.

Brazil's coach also turned to a scrawny 17-year-old kid, born Edson Arantes do Nascimento—better known as Pelé. At the time, he was the youngest person to play at a World Cup. He didn't look like much, but he sure could play soccer. In fact, he was already playing as a professional. Pelé would become known as the greatest soccer player of all time.

Brazil beat the Soviet Union. Then in the semifinals against France, Pelé went up against Fontaine. Fontaine scored once, but Pelé got a hat trick. Brazil would meet Sweden in the finals. Here Pelé scored two more goals. For the second, Pelé controlled a high ball with his chest before letting it fall onto his foot and kicking it into the goal. It was perhaps the most impressive two seconds of soccer the sport had ever seen. In 1958, the World Cup was broadcast internationally for the first time. Pelé's goal was seen on television around the world. That moment helped give Brazil its first World Cup championship—and Pelé a place in history.

Brazil was a heavy favorite going into the 1962 World Cup in Chile. However, the team faced battle after battle. In an early game against Mexico, Pelé tore his hamstring and was out for the rest of

In 1966, England's Geoff Hurst secured an extra-time win with this controversial goal. The ball bounced off the crossbar, only briefly crossing into the goal.

the tournament. Garrincha was injured in the semifinals against Chile. However, in the final against Czechoslovakia, the Brazilian team showed the skill and instinct they had brought out in 1958. This time they were shaped by four more years of experience. Brazil notched up its second championship.

ENGLAND IN 1966

Despite England's great history with soccer, the country did not host a World Cup until 1966. The English team was loaded with talent that year. Even so, the country did not seem terribly excited. To help promote the event, the World Cup got its first mascot—a lion named World Cup Willie.

Brazil, led by Pelé, was as strong as ever. Also getting a lot of attention was Portugal. Their powerful forward, Eusébio, was the sport's first great African player. He is still ranked as one of the greatest players of the century. In an early match against Bulgaria, Pelé was hurt. When it came time for Brazil to play Portugal, the injured Pelé was not up to the challenge of Eusébio. Portugal won.

Portugal then played North Korea. North Korea scored three times in only 20 minutes. However, in an astonishing display, Eusébio scored five straight goals for his team. Portugal left the field with a 5–3 victory. Portugal was finally stopped in the semi-final against England.

The finals featured England against West Germany. The teams tied 2–2 and went into extra time. English player Geoff Hurst sent the ball flying toward the West German goal. It hit the top bar, shot straight down, and bounced back onto the field. Had it crossed the invisible line to put it into the goal? It was a controversial call, but the referee ruled in favor of England. The tie was broken. Minutes later, Hurst scored again, getting a hat trick. It was the first ever in a final.

CHAPTER 3

THE 1970s:
BRAZIL TAKES THE CUP HOME

The original World Cup itself, the Jules Rimet trophy, was 40 years old. It had traveled to five different countries but never more than twice. That was about to end.

A BEAUTIFUL END

In 1970, Brazil once again entered the World Cup as a team stacked with talent. Pelé had been treated very roughly on the field four years earlier. He threatened not to return to the Cup but then changed his mind.

Italy and England also had strong teams. And West Germany had the powerful Gerd Müller. He was nicknamed "Der Bomber" ("the bomber"). He wasn't a well-rounded player, but he could do one important thing: put the ball into the net.

In the quarterfinals, England took an early lead, but West Germany tied things up. The match went into extra time. Müller then scored his eighth goal of the tournament. It gave West Germany the win and pushed the team into the semifinals.

That's when things really got interesting. The semifinal between West Germany and Italy came to be known as the "Game of the Century." Both teams had two World Cup titles. Italy was ahead for most of the match, but then West Germany's Karl Heinz Schnellinger tied the game right at the end. Adding to the drama was the fact that Schnellinger played professional soccer for an Italian team.

The game went into extra time, and the players poured on extra effort. The ball flew back and forth as the two teams scored a total of five goals in the next few minutes. But the clock ran out eventually, and when it did, Italy had won.

Italy was into the finals for the first time in more than 30 years. Now they faced Brazil, an awesome force in the world of soccer. Italy was known for their superb defense. However, if anyone could bust through the wall of Italian players, it was Brazil. Italy held on through the first half. However, by the second half, they were beginning to weaken. Calmly and steadily, Brazil played great soccer. It wasn't nasty or rough, like so many matches in the previous decade. Instead, their game shone with skill and teamwork. It was a "beautiful game." The Italians' 4–1 loss was not unexpected. However, it was nothing to be ashamed of. The Brazilian team was considered by many to be the best soccer team ever.

This was Brazil's third World Cup win. With it, the Jules Rimet trophy was retired. It was awarded one final time to Brazil.

NEW BEGINNINGS

FIFA had a new trophy made for the 1974 World Cup in West Germany. It was made out of gold and cost about $20,000.

Along with the new trophy came a new style of soccer. The Dutch (people who live in Holland) had pioneered a playing style called "total soccer." In earlier years, the playing positions were well established. Offensive players scored goals. Defensive players prevented goals. They worked in certain parts of the field. Players did their jobs and stayed where they were supposed to.

Total soccer changed everything. The Dutch blended the play. Boundaries between positions became blurred. Players switched positions easily. This confused players on the other team, who were supposed to guard them. They did not know exactly what

WORLD CUP MEXICO 1970

WINNER
BRAZIL

FINAL STADIUM/CITY
AZTECA/MEXICO CITY

FINAL SCORE
BRAZIL 4, ITALY 1

GOLDEN SHOE WINNER
GERD MULLER,
W. GERMANY (10)

PARTICIPANTS
16

MATCHES
32

NUMBER OF GOALS/AVERAGE
95/3.0

NUMBER OF SPECTATORS/AVERAGE
1,603,975 / 50,124

Brazil's Pelé waits for Italy's Gigi Riva to come down after a header during the 1970 finals. Brazil took a 4–1 victory in the "beautiful game."

their opponents were up to. With this new style, the players could easily get to where the action was and create a way to score. Players who could do this were versatile in both mind and body. They could think of creative plays and pull off the physical moves needed to make them happen. This style of playing was enough for Holland to dominate in the early rounds.

There were other firsts at the 1974 Cup. West Germany faced its neighbor and political opposite, East Germany, then a Communist nation. The two teams met in the first round. It was the first time the two countries had played each other since Germany had been divided in World War II. (They would unite as a single team again in 1990.) East Germany took a surprising win. That turned out to be a stroke of luck for West Germany. The loss kept them from facing powerhouses Holland and Brazil in the next stage. West Germany survived until the final match against Holland.

The 1974 World Cup introduced a new gold trophy to replace the Jules Rimet trophy. Italian designer Silvio Gazzaniga said he wanted it to show "power and energy."

WORLD CUP GERMANY 1974

WINNER
W. GERMANY

FINAL STADIUM/CITY
OLYMPIASTADION/MUNICH

FINAL SCORE
W. GERMANY 2, HOLLAND 1

GOLDEN SHOE WINNER
GRZEGORZ LATO, POLAND (7)

PARTICIPANTS
16

MATCHES
38

NUMBER OF GOALS/AVERAGE
97/2.6

NUMBER OF SPECTATORS/AVERAGE
1,768,152 / 46,530

The final saw some early action. The clock had not even run a minute when Holland scored on a penalty kick. West Germany had not even touched the ball, and already they were behind! However, the team was known for coming back when they were down. Holland paid close attention to its defense, but it was not enough. The West Germans managed to put two balls into the net. The second one was scored by West Germany's Gerd Müller. It proved to be the last of the game. Although both teams played smart, exciting soccer for the second half, it did not result in any goals. Holland kept waiting for an opportunity, but West Germany skillfully denied them. The win went to the host, West Germany.

Holland's Johan Cruyff (right) mastered the team's style of "total football" in 1974, and helped his country win this match against Uruguay. Holland lost in the finals to

ARGENTINA'S BOLD MOVE

International politics had always been a part of the World Cup, and in 1978, they again took a starring role. When Argentina was chosen to host the tournament, one government was in charge. But then the government was overthrown, and the army put a new government into power. The new government brought terrorism and violence. Many countries around the world criticized Argentina. FIFA considered moving the tournament but, in the end, decided to stay with Argentina.

In the soccer world, Argentina's coach was also being criticized. Worldwide, most countries wanted their best players to make up the national team. Sometimes, those players were playing for clubs in other countries. Often, they would return to their home country to train for the World Cup.

Argentina's coach took a different approach. He decided to use "local" players who were already playing in the country's professional leagues. Some people thought this was a bad idea. He was passing up some of Argentina's best players.

The coach did make one exception to his rule. That was for Mario Kempes. Kempes was an Argentine who played in a Spanish club. He was the one player asked to come home for the World Cup.

The coach's strategy was to emphasize ball skills,

WORLD CUP ARGENTINA 1978

Argentina '78

WINNER
ARGENTINA

FINAL STADIUM/CITY
MONUMENTAL/
BUENOS AIRES

FINAL SCORE
ARGENTINA 3, HOLLAND 1

GOLDEN SHOE WINNER
MARIO KEMPES,
ARGENTINA (6)

PARTICIPANTS
16

MATCHES
38

NUMBER OF GOALS/AVERAGE
102/2.7

NUMBER OF SPECTATORS/AVERAGE
1,546,151 / 40,688

Confetti litters the pitch as Argentina's Mario Kempes welcomes cheers from the fans. Kempes led Argentina to a 3–1 victory over Holland in the 1978 World Cup.

such as dribbling, rather than physical dominance. Critics called it "fulbito" ("little football"). They thought it was a weak approach.

They were almost proven right. Argentina barely squeaked through the early rounds. However, the team's approach came together in an electric game against Peru. They won and gained a place in the finals against Holland.

The final was full of furious offense, although the score stayed relatively low. Regulation ended in a 1–1 tie, with Kempes scoring Argentina's goal. In extra time, Kempes scored again and then set up another goal, which put the final score at 3–1. In the minds of fans, Argentina's coach went from stupid to smart. His "local" strategy had paid off.

The political mood of Argentina was divisive. But for a few days in 1978, both the government and the people agreed on one thing: the glory of Argentina's victory.

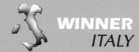

THE 1980s AND 1990s:
MARADONA'S TIME

Argentina's Diego Maradona did not burst onto the scene as Pelé had in 1958. Instead, Maradona made only a brief appearance in his 1982 debut. Those who forgot him were to be reminded four years later. Maradona defined the 1986 World Cup more than any single player since Pelé.

ITALY'S COMEBACK

Italy dominated the World Cup in the 1930s. But for the next 40 years, the Italians could not bring home a championship. For the 1982 World Cup in Spain, the Italians had a solid team. However, they lacked the one thing they needed to win games: someone they could depend on to kick the ball into the net. The Italian coach turned to Paolo Rossi.

Rossi had played for the Italian team in 1978 and was an accomplished professional. In 1980, however, he got mixed up in a scandal. He was accused of helping to "fix" matches, meaning that certain teams were paid to lose. (People would do this in order to make sure they won gambling bets.) Rossi said he was innocent. However, he was banned

WORLD CUP SPAIN 1982

WINNER
ITALY

FINAL STADIUM/CITY
ESTADIO SANTIAGO BERNABÉU/MADRID

FINAL SCORE
ITALY 3, W. GERMANY 1

GOLDEN SHOE WINNER
PAOLO ROSSI, ITALY (6)

GOLDEN BALL WINNER
PAOLO ROSSI, ITALY

PARTICIPANTS
24

MATCHES
52

NUMBER OF GOALS/AVERAGE
146/2.8

NUMBER OF SPECTATORS/AVERAGE
2,109,723 / 40,571

from soccer for two years. Luckily for Italy, his suspension ended just in time for the World Cup in 1982.

In the early rounds, Rossi's play was unremarkable. But still Italy moved up. That's when Rossi started to show his talent. When Italy met Brazil in the quarterfinals, Rossi scored a hat trick. The third was the winning goal. Against Poland in the semifinals, he scored both of Italy's goals.

On other fields at the World Cup, France was drawing attention. The team did not advance to the finals. However, they stood out because of the highly skilled play of Michel Platini, the French team captain. He was able to power his team through the opening rounds.

France's semifinal against Germany was one of the greatest matches of 1982, a hard-fought battle that was ultimately decided in a penalty shoot-out. However, it is most remembered for one horrible moment. The German goalkeeper, Harald Schumacher, knocked a French player unconscious. Schumacher was allowed to continue playing. Fans were outraged. France, who eventually lost, had to play not knowing if their teammate was alive.

The finals featured Italy against West Germany. There were two European teams, playing on European soil, but the fans were not evenly split. Still angry over the Schumacher incident, most Europeans were rooting for Italy.

The game stayed scoreless for a while. When a number finally went up on the board, it went to Italy. It came—again—from Rossi. Two other players brought Italy's total to three. West Germany scored only once. Italy had its third World Cup win.

WORLD CUP MEXICO 1986

WINNER
ARGENTINA

FINAL STADIUM/CITY
AZTECA/MEXICO CITY

FINAL SCORE
ARGENTINA 3,
W. GERMANY 2

GOLDEN SHOE WINNER
GARY LINEKER,
ENGLAND (6)

GOLDEN BALL WINNER
DIEGO A. MARADONA, ARGENTINA

FAIR PLAY
BRAZIL

PARTICIPANTS
24

MATCHES
52

NUMBER OF GOALS/AVERAGE
132/2.5

NUMBER OF SPECTATORS/AVERAGE
2,393,331 / 46,025

MARADONA MAGIC

Argentina was knocked out early in 1982, so spectators got only a glimpse of the team's star, Diego Maradona. When the Cup returned to Mexico for the 1986 tournament, however, he would stun the crowds.

As leaders from Mexico and West Germany watch, Argentina's Diego Maradona embraces the World Cup trophy in 1986. Maradona's play during the tournament was both brilliant and controversial.

Maradona's moves—the good and the bad—were on full display in the quarterfinal against England. In the second half, Maradona lunged to intercept a pass. He collided with England's goalkeeper. The ball went into the goal, but the play was messy and confusing. No one seemed sure what had happened. The referee ruled that the goal was good. Maradona later said the goal came from the "hand of God." People who watched a video replay agreed that the goal came from someone's hand—Maradona's! He had hit the ball into the net. The goal was illegal, but it was too late now.

Just three minutes later in the game, Maradona showed his real skills. He took the ball down the field, past five of England's defenders, on a 70-yard run that ended in a neat kick into England's goal. This play was voted the greatest ever at a World Cup, called the "Goal of the Century." Argentina won the quarter-finals, and then the semifinals, and then the final match against West Germany. But it wasn't the win people talked about—it was those few minutes Maradona took to make World Cup history.

Maradona's "hand of God" goal caused a lot of controversy. As a result, FIFA started the Fair Play program. This program was designed to get people to obey the rules and show respect to other players. FIFA gives the Fair Play Award to individual players, organizations, and fans who have shown sportsmanlike behavior.

NEW KIDS ON THE BLOCK

For almost 50 years, the World Cup had been a tournament for Europe, South America, and Latin America. That began to change in the late 1970s, when Africa began fielding competitive teams.

In 1978, a team from Tunisia competed. When they beat Mexico, they became the first African team to win a match at the World Cup. They also played another team to a tie. That team was West Germany, the reigning World Cup champions. For people who felt the World Cup should include more African countries, this game was proof that African countries could hold their own.

In 1982, Cameroon made an appearance. Like Tunisia, the team did not advance past the first round, but they held Peru, Poland, and

Roger Milla played for African country Cameroon in the 1982 World Cup games. Here, he wrestles with Italian Giancarlo Antognoni for the ball. The little-known team

Italy to tie scores. In 1986, Morocco entered the tournament. They beat Portugal, which let them enter the second round.

In 1990, Cameroon and Egypt now represented the African continent. With only nine players, Cameroon beat Argentina. The team eventually got to the quarterfinals against England. No African country had ever gotten so far. Although Cameroon lost, the fans admired their spunk.

Also starting to put in an appearance at the Cup was another country from the Americas—the United States. The United States hadn't been seen at the Cup for 40 years, even though the team had a considerable history in the World Cup. The team finished in third place in Uruguay in 1930, and it was an American player, Bert Patenaude, who was the first to score a hat trick in a World Cup final in that same tournament. The U.S. team lost all of their early round games in 1990, but they were back in 1994, hosting the tournament for the first time. A lot of people did not think the United States should get to host the tournament. But they proved to be a good host. Soccer got its largest audiences ever, both in the stands and on TV. On the field, the performance of the U.S. team was also considered a success. They exited the tournament after

WORLD CUP ITALY 1990

ITALIA 90

WINNER
WEST GERMANY

FINAL STADIUM/CITY
OLIMPICO/ROME

FINAL SCORE
W. GERMANY 1,
ARGENTINA 0

GOLDEN SHOE WINNER
SALVATORE SCHILLACI,
ITALY (6)

GOLDEN BALL WINNER
SALVATORE SCHILLACI,
ITALY

FAIR PLAY
ENGLAND

PARTICIPANTS
24

MATCHES
52

NUMBER OF GOALS/AVERAGE
115/2.2

NUMBER OF SPECTATORS/AVERAGE
2,516,348 / 48,391

Salvatore Schillaci (front) tries to stay ahead of U.S. player Jimmy Banks in this 1990 match. The United States lost, but fans were happy to see the team at the World Cup for the first time since 1950.

a tense battle with eventual winner Brazil in the knockout stage. The 1994 World Cup marked a few firsts. The match between the host and Switzerland at the Pontiac Silverdome was the first indoor game in World Cup history, although it was played on natural grass. The final match, between Brazil and Italy, at the Rose Bowl in Pasadena, California, was the first to be decided on a penalty shoot-out after no goals had been scored in regular time or in extra time. With this victory, Brazil became the first country in history to win four World Cup titles.

PATRIOTS OF SOCCER

In France 1998, the World Cup expanded to 32 teams. This meant there were more games and more nations playing for the first time in the competition. Japan, Jamaica, South Africa, and Croatia debuted with different levels of success. Japan found themselves with three consecutive losses, one against Jamaica. The Jamaicans were also playing their first World Cup, and this was their first and only victory. South Africa lost their first game against the hosts, but tied their next two games against Denmark and Saudi Arabia. Yet South Africa failed to advance to the second round. Croatia was

WORLD CUP USA 1994

WINNER
BRAZIL

FINAL STADIUM/CITY
ROSE BOWL/PASADENA

FINAL SCORE
*BRAZIL 0, ITALY 0
(BRAZIL 3–2 PSO)*

GOLDEN SHOE WINNER
*OLEG SALENKO,
RUSSIA (6)
HRISTO STOICHKOV,
BULGARIA (6)*

GOLDEN BALL WINNER
ROMARIO, BRAZIL

FAIR PLAY
BRAZIL

PARTICIPANTS
24

MATCHES
52

NUMBER OF GOALS/AVERAGE
141/2.7

NUMBER OF SPECTATORS/AVERAGE
3,587,538 / 68,991

Scoreless soccer was the theme at the 1994 finals in California, which came down to a penalty shoot-out. Here, Italy's Roberto Baggio misses a shot, leaving Italy with only two points to Brazil's three.

a different story. They moved easily in their first round, and a 1–0 win against Romania sent them to the quarterfinals against powerful Germany. The Croatian national team was formed just eight years before, shortly before the country's independence from Yugoslavia, and beating the powerful German team seemed an impossible mission. However, the Croatians prevailed in a 3–0 victory and advanced to the semifinal against the hosts. Croatia lost the game but finished in third place. Not bad for a debuting team.

The global nature of soccer was obvious on France's 1998 team. Their players came from all over—not just France. Zinédine Zidane, the team's star, was born in France but had Algerian parents. The French people didn't seem too excited about their multinational team.

However, the World Cup was being played in France, and it gave the team a home advantage. France beat South Africa, Saudi Arabia, Denmark, and Paraguay. The French people began to pay attention now that France was winning. The quarterfinals saw Italy fall. Croatia went down in the semifinals. France was in the finals—against Brazil.

By now, the French had become supremely interested in soccer. Brazil, with its long tradition of soccer, was a favorite in the 1998 tournament. Somehow France had earned a place opposite them.

WORLD CUP FRANCE 1998

COUPE DU MONDE

FRANCE 98

WINNER
FRANCE

FINAL STADIUM/CITY
STADE ST. DENIS/PARIS

FINAL SCORE
FRANCE 3, BRAZIL 0

GOLDEN SHOE WINNER
DAVOR SUKER,
CROATIA (6)

GOLDEN BALL WINNER
RONALDO, BRAZIL

FAIR PLAY
ENGLAND, FRANCE

PARTICIPANTS
32

MATCHES
64

NUMBER OF GOALS/AVERAGE
171/2.7

NUMBER OF SPECTATORS/AVERAGE
2,785,100 / 43,517

French player Zinédine Zidane leads France to a 3–0 victory against Brazil in 1998. The French people went into the World Cup unexcited, but came out huge fans of their national team.

Brazil's star, Ronaldo, played badly in the final match. He had been having convulsions only hours before the tournament. This little chink in Brazil's armor was enough for France. Zidane scored twice in the first half. Another goal in the second half gave them a 3–0 victory. France had once shrugged at their multinational team. Now it celebrated these same players. For the win, everyone was French.

CHAPTER 5

THE 2000s:
THE CUP TRAVELS TO ASIA

I n 2002, the Cup went to Asia and crossed into new territory. For the second year of the second millennium, two nations—South Korea and Japan—took on the job of hosting the World Cup.

Was Africa next in line? For 2006, FIFA representatives had to vote between South Africa and Germany. It looked as if South Africa would win. However, one FIFA member who favored South Africa did not vote. This controversial choice confused many and angered some. But no one could argue with the numbers. Germany had won by one vote. South Africa would have to wait.

WORLD CUP KOREA/JAPAN 2002

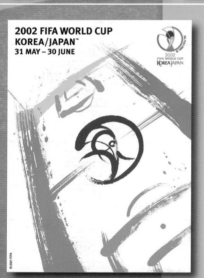

2002 FIFA WORLD CUP KOREA/JAPAN™
31 MAY – 30 JUNE

WINNER
BRAZIL

FINAL STADIUM/CITY
YOKOHAMA INTERNATIONAL STADIUM/ YOKOHAMA, JAPAN

FINAL SCORE
BRAZIL 2, GERMANY 0

GOLDEN SHOE WINNER
RONALDO, BRAZIL (8)

GOLDEN BALL WINNER
OLIVER KAHN, GERMANY

FAIR PLAY
BELGIUM

PARTICIPANTS
32

MATCHES
64

NUMBER OF GOALS/AVERAGE
161/2.5

NUMBER OF SPECTATORS/AVERAGE
2,705,197 / 42,269

TWO FOR '02

Having two hosts was a first for the World Cup. Historically, South Korea and Japan had been political enemies. It was so bad that half a century earlier, the South Koreans refused to let a Japanese soccer team cross the South Korean border to play. The two countries' partnership in 2002 was a historic display of cooperation.

This was the first time the World Cup had been played in Asia. But it was not just the choice of host countries that showed soccer was becoming even more international. At the 2002 tournament, the colors on the jerseys and the

Brazil's Ronaldo clutches the national flag as he rides on a teammate's shoulders after Brazil's 2–0 win over Germany in 2002. Ronaldo deserved to get his feet off the ground after scoring both of Brazil's goals.

names on the scoreboard showed that more countries than ever were participating. Slovenia, China, Senegal, and Turkey did not traditionally have a presence at the World Cup.

In addition, countries that didn't usually do that well were performing like never before. The United States, still relatively new to soccer, beat Mexico before losing to Germany in the quarter-finals. Cohost South Korea made it all the way to the semifinals before Germany took them out.

Senegal and Turkey both reached the quarter-finals, where they played each other. Turkey lost in the semifinals, but they left with a third-place finish overall. Fans were treated to great soccer from Turkey, as well as from South Korea, who was awarded the prize for the "most entertaining" team.

Although South Korea and Turkey advanced to the semifinals, both the finalists ended up being soccer veterans. Brazil met Germany for the final match of the 2002 World Cup. Four years earlier, Brazil had suffered a huge loss at the hands of the French. Their star, Ronaldo, had not played as well as he was expected to. By 2002, Ronaldo was ready to redeem himself. He proved his reputation by

WORLD CUP GERMANY 2006

WINNER
ITALY

FINAL STADIUM/CITY
BERLIN OLYMPIC STADIUM/BERLIN

FINAL SCORE
ITALY 1, FRANCE 1 (ITALY 5–3 PSO)

GOLDEN SHOE WINNER
MIROSLAV KLOSE, GERMANY (5)

GOLDEN BALL WINNER
ZINÉDINE ZIDANE, FRANCE

FAIR PLAY
SPAIN, BRAZIL

PARTICIPANTS
32

MATCHES
64

NUMBER OF GOALS/AVERAGE
147/2.3

NUMBER OF SPECTATORS/AVERAGE
3,359,439 / 52,491

Cristiano Ronaldo (left) shows why he's Portugal's star as he delivers some fancy foot-
work and holds off Russia's Alexey Smertin in 2006. The young player is popular but

scoring both goals for Brazil in the 2–0 victory over Germany. With this win, Brazil notched its total World Cup wins up to five. They had more wins than any other country.

RISING STARS

The most spectacular players aren't always on the winning team. France's Just Fontaine, the highest all-time scorer in a single World Cup tournament, was not. Nor was Portugal's Eusébio or France's Michel Platini. In 2002, it was the second-place team, Germany, who had striker Miroslav Klose. This was Klose's first World Cup.

Klose scored five goals in the tournament, all of them headers. After scoring, he celebrated by doing a flip on the field. His enthusiasm was contagious. The German fans nicknamed him "Salto-Klose" for his somersaults.

Klose was back at the 2006 World Cup. This one was held in his home country. He was more than a fan favorite. He was practically a national hero. Again, "Salto" scored five goals. (This time, only one was a header.) He was the only player to have scored five goals at two consecutive World Cups. In 2006, this was enough to earn him the Golden Shoe Award for the highest scorer at the tournament.

The 2006 World Cup introduced still more stars. Cristiano Ronaldo came from Portugal. (He should not be confused with the Brazilian player known simply as "Ronaldo.") Cristiano Ronaldo played professionally for England, although for the World Cup, he played for his home country.

Ronaldo scored only one goal at the 2006 Cup. However, he made headlines after a match against England. It started when English player Wayne Rooney made a particularly rough move against another Portuguese player. Ronaldo objected. Rooney pushed him and was expelled from the game. Right after this incident, Ronaldo winked at his teammates. The English fans were furious. FIFA got a flood of e-mails from English fans—and it was not good. At the time, FIFA was in the process of gathering names for the Best Young Player award. Cristiano Ronaldo was clearly

To the delight of fans in Berlin, Germany's Miroslav Klose executes his trademark somersault after scoring during a match with Ecuador in 2006. His five goals during the tournament earned him the title of highest scorer.

one of the best young players, but his name was left off the list. FIFA admitted that his behavior, and the negative publicity surrounding him, were part of the decision.

However, after the 2006 World Cup, Ronaldo continued to play excellent soccer. In 2008, he won the award for Best Soccer Player in Europe.

Another young star, Lionel Messi, came from Argentina. He had been injured shortly before the 2006 World Cup and almost didn't make the national team. When he did, he played in only one match against Serbia. For the quarterfinals against Germany, he sat on the bench, looking disappointed and upset.

But Messi was only 19 years old at the 2006 tournament. He still has a career in front of him. He is consistently ranked as one of the world's best soccer players. He also got a boost from Argentine soccer legend Diego Maradona. Maradona said, "I have seen the player who will inherit my place in Argentine football, and his name is Messi."

ITALIAN TEAMWORK

Who would play at the 2006 World Cup? There's always a question about which teams will make it through. In 2006, the question seemed to be less about which teams would play than which players would still be standing. Rough play marked the entire tournament. When a player gets too rough, he receives a red card and is thrown out of the game. The referees were handing them out at a record pace.

This trend continued into the finals, where France met Italy. In regulation time, the two teams played to a 1–1 tie. Tensions ran high in extra time. French player Zinédine Zidane and Italy's Marco Materazzi got into an argument. Zidane head-butted Materazzi in the chest. The referee gave Zidane a red card, and he had to leave the game. He became the first player to be expelled in a World Cup final. Later, the two players each offered their version of what had happened, but it was never clear exactly what was said. At the time it didn't matter. Zidane was France's star, and he was out just when his team needed him most.

Italy's star in 2006 was the whole team. The squad's 5–3 victory was a group effort, which shows as players and coaches celebrate together on the field.

A furious battle of penalty kicks came next. By the time it ended, the ball had crossed the goal line six times. Italy came out on top, with a final score of 5–3. Italy had its fourth World Cup win.

Despite the ugliness in the last minutes of the final, Italy deserved the title. If ever a win came through sheer teamwork, Italy's 2006 victory was it. Out of 23 players who came with Italy's national team, 21 played. Ten different players scored throughout the tournament, proving that Italy needed all of their players' various skills. There will always be individual stars who capture the fans' imagination, but no one player wins a game. The 2006 games proved that.

D espite Africa's contributions to soccer, a World Cup had never been held on the African continent. It was time to change that.

South Africa had lost the 2006 Cup by only one vote. Although disappointed, South African officials regrouped and set their sights on 2010. Four other African nations also decided to try. They were Egypt, Libya, Morocco, and Tunisia. This time there was no nail-bitingly close race. South Africa won with an overwhelming 14 votes.

THE POLITICS OF SOUTH AFRICA

South Africa is located at the southern tip of the African continent. It has a large mix of people, including blacks, whites, Indians, Asians, and people of mixed races. The country has 11 official languages!

In 1948, South Africa began a social and political practice known as apartheid. This system segregated blacks from whites. Although most people in South Africa were black, they were governed by white people. The whites did not always treat the blacks fairly. The country was suspended and later expelled as a member of FIFA.

Nelson Mandela was a South African political activist who fought against apartheid in the 1950s. He was arrested for defying the government, and in 1962, he was sent to jail. He stayed there for the next 27 years. Finally, in 1990, South Africa began to do away with apartheid. Mandela was freed. In 1994, South Africa held its first democratic election, and Mandela was elected as the country's president.

Because of his support of equality for black people, Mandela became a national and global hero. He won the Nobel Peace Prize in 1993.

When South Africa was chosen to host the World Cup, Mandela was there. His happiness showed as he clutched the World Cup trophy and wept at the announcement. However, the compassion that had guided his life was still there. He said

South African hero and leader Nelson Mandela clutches the World Cup trophy in an emotional moment after South Africa won the right to host the 2010 World Cup.

to the losing countries, "You must not be discouraged. It is no reflection of your efforts. Next time when you compete, you may be luckier." He added, "South Africans should treat this decision with humility and without arrogance because we are, after all, equal."

An Egyptian journalist stood up and said, "We love you, Nelson Mandela."

Mandela represented the spirit of equality. It was fitting that he held the trophy when Africa joined Europe, Asia, and the Americas in the right to host the World Cup.

PREPARATIONS

It was in 2004 that FIFA voted for South Africa to host in 2010. The country had six years to get ready. It seemed like a long time, but there was a lot of work to do. They were getting ready for a party that would last a month and have millions of guests! They needed to do a lot more than just stock up on chips and soda.

For one thing, South Africa needed to improve the country's infrastructure. Infrastructure includes the things that help a country operate. Water and power supplies are part of a country's infrastructure. So are roads and other transportation systems.

Nine cities across South Africa would host matches. They needed to build stadiums. They had to make sure there were thousands of hotel rooms available. By 2007, FIFA officials seemed concerned. Progress was slow. Stadiums were not getting finished. Would South Africa be ready in time? Or did FIFA need to find another host? FIFA president Sepp Blatter said he was sticking to the original plan. The World Cup would be held in South Africa. However, he admitted that another nation could step in if necessary. Germany was prepared from hosting in 2006. England and the United States also had the facilities.

However, by 2008, construction was moving forward. It appeared South Africa would be ready. At least, it would be physically ready. But was it mentally ready? At the end of 2008, Blatter had another complaint. He said South Africans did not

In a blur of color, South African player Teko Modise demonstrates his skill during a qualifying match for the 2010 tournament. As the host country, South Africa is guar-

appear enthusiastic about the event. "I'm missing the feeling of the World Cup," he said. "Africa needs to tell the world it's ready to host the event."

Now South Africa had to work on its mental infrastructure!

THE COMPETITION

There is a saying in soccer that the British invented football, but the Brazilians perfected it. In truth, as soccer has developed over the last century, many different countries have developed their own styles and strategies. The British are known for their straightforward, waste-no-time approach. The Germans are forceful and organized. The Italians are known for being strong defenders. Players in Latin and South America have top-notch ball skills. Holland's "total football" emphasized versatility.

No one style of play is best. At different times, against different opponents, each has its advantages and disadvantages. Because soccer is played so widely around the world, it changes constantly. A team that seemed unbeatable four years ago may now struggle. Underdog teams may suddenly come together and play highly competitive soccer.

Qualifying matches for the 2010 World Cup began in 2008. There are a total of 32 slots. South Africa, because it is the host nation, is guaranteed one space. However, South Africa's home team, Bafana Bafana, is not strong. The team did not qualify for the African Nations Cup in 2010.

The other 31 slots are filled by playoffs. A record 204 countries competed for these spaces. The previous record was set in 2002, when 199 teams competed.

A UNIFYING FORCE

In 2007, statesman Nelson Mandela watched a soccer match played in his honor. He said, "[This game] symbolizes the power of football to bring people together from all over the world, regardless of the language they speak or the color of their skin."

Children pose with Zakumi, the green-haired leopard that is the mascot for the 2010 games. Zakumi's name is a blend of "ZA"—the abbreviation for South Africa, and "kumi," which means "10" in several African languages.

Although South Africa has emerged from the dark tunnel of apartheid, the country still has problems. In October 2008, South Africa's government forced its president, Thabo Mbeki, out of office. Two months later, supporters of Mbeki formed a new political party. This one opposed the African National Congress (ANC). With a major split in the government, South Africa's politics were fragile.

Security is another issue at the games. The country has a high rate of gun violence. Some people worry that the country cannot make sure that thousands of visitors will be safe. In answer, South Africa has hired thousands more police to work during the month-long World Cup.

The motto for the 2010 games is "Celebrate Africa's Humanity." Supporters of the tournament hope that it will prove the country has moved away from the dark days of apartheid.

The head of South Africa's organizing committee for the World Cup is Dr. Irvin Khoza. He said, "Football has played a huge role in bringing unity to South Africa and now more than ever we must show our responsibility as a nation, as a football family, and as a host of the World Cup."

Politics has always played a part in soccer. But people play a bigger part. Millions of people smash into one country. They fill the streets and the stands. There is no room to be divided. Not at the World Cup.

GLOSSARY

apartheid A social system that separates blacks and whites and makes blacks inferior.

brawny Large and strong.

consecutive Two or more things coming in a row, with nothing in between.

consistent Reliable; relatively unchanging.

defy To resist or oppose.

dire Warning of danger or disaster.

dominate To show force or superiority.

fluke An incident that is accidental and results in a surprising outcome.

hamstring A tendon in the thigh that connects muscle to bone.

inherit To receive something from someone who will no longer use it.

javelin A spear.

lunge To throw one's entire body at something.

mascot A cartoonlike character designed to represent a specific team or event.

outraged Feeling furious because of an unfair situation.

regroup To reorganize or put back in order.

reigning To be currently in power or recognized as a champion.

trounce To beat someone thoroughly in a game.

underdog A competitor who is considered unlikely to win.

veteran Someone with previous experience in an activity.

American Youth Soccer Organization
National Support & Training Center
12501 S. Isis Avenue
Hawthorne, CA 90250
(800) 872-2976
Web site: http://soccer.org/home.aspx
This organization administers youth recreational soccer leagues all over the country.
    Any skill level is welcome.

Canadian Soccer Association
Place Soccer Canada
237 Metcalfe Street
Ottawa, ON K2P 1R2
Canada
(613) 237-7678
E-mail: mini@soccercan.ca
Web site: http://www.canadasoccer.com
The Canadian Soccer Association works to promote soccer and improve the game at
    both the national and international levels.

CONCACAF
725 Fifth Avenue, Floor 17
New York, NY 10022
(212) 308-0044
E-mail: contact@concacaf.org
Web site: http://www.concacaf.com
With 40 member countries, the Confederation of North, Central America, and
    Caribbean Association Football oversees soccer for these regions. It is one of six
    divisions of FIFA.

FIFA
FIFA-Strasse 20
P.O. Box 8044

Zurich, Switzerland
+41-(0)43 222 7777
Web site: http://www.fifa.com
FIFA is the international organization that oversees soccer at the professional level. It
    sponsors the World Cup.

National Soccer Hall of Fame
18 Stadium Circle
Oneonta, NY 13820
(607) 432-3351
E-mail: nshof@soccerhall.org
Web site: http://www.soccerhall.org
The National Soccer Hall of Fame preserves and promotes the history of soccer in the
    United States.

U.S. Soccer Federation
1801 S. Prairie Avenue
Chicago, IL 60616
(312) 808-1300
Web site: http://www.ussoccer.com
The U.S. Soccer Federation oversees both professional and amateur soccer and helps
    promote and develop the sport.

WEB SITES

Due to the changing nature of Internet links, Rosen Publishing has developed an online
list of Web sites related to the subject of this book. This site is updated regularly. Please
use this link to access the list:

http://www.rosenlinks.com/wsb/wcup

FOR FURTHER READING

Buckley, James. *Pelé*. New York, NY: DK Children, 2007.

Buxton, Ted. *Soccer Skills: For Young Players*. Richmond Hill, Ontario, Canada: Firefly Books, 2007.

Crouch, Terry. *The World Cup: The Complete History*. London, England: Aurum Press, Ltd., 2006.

Esckilsen, Erik. *Offsides*. New York, NY: Houghton Mifflin Books for Children, 2004.

Fiore, Fernando. *The World Cup: The Ultimate Guide to the Greatest Sports Spectacle in the World*. New York, NY: HarperCollins Publishers, 2006.

Fitzgerald, Dawn. *Soccer Chick Rules*. New York, NY: Square Fish, 2007.

Gifford, Clive. *The Kingfisher Soccer Encyclopedia*. New York, NY: Kingfisher, 2006.

Hornby, Hugh. *Soccer*. New York, NY: DK Children, 2008.

Hunt, Chris. *The Complete Book of Soccer*. Buffalo, NY: Firefly Books, 2006.

Lisi, Clemente Angelo. *A History of the World Cup: 1930–2006*. Lanham, MD: Scarecrow Press, Inc., 2007.

Miers, Charles, and Elio Trifari, eds. *Soccer! The Game and the World Cup*. New York, NY: Rizzoli International Publications, 1994.

Rigby, Robert. *Goal! The Dream Begins*. New York, NY: Harcourt Paperbacks, 2006.

Stewart, Mark. *The World Cup*. New York, NY: Franklin Watts, 2003.

Whitfield, David. *World Cup*. New York, NY: Weigl Publishers, 2007.

BBC Sport. "Blatter Calls for 2010 Enthusiasm." September 17, 2008. Retrieved February 22, 2009 (http://news.bbc.co.uk/sport2/hi/football/africa/7621544.stm).

BBC Sport. "FIFA Makes 2010 Cup Back-up Plan." April 30, 2007. Retrieved February 22, 2009 (http://news.bbc.co.uk/sport2/hi/football/internationals/6606725.stm).

Crouch, Terry. *The World Cup: The Complete History.* London, England: Aurum Press, Ltd., 2006.

ExpertFootball.com. "Soccer Styles of Play." Retrieved February 28, 2009 (http://expertfootball.com/coaching/styles.php).

FIFA.com. "FIFA Fair Play." Retrieved March 6, 2009 (http://www.fifa.com/aboutfifa/worldwideprograms/footballforhope/fairplay/index.html).

FIFA.com. "The History of FIFA." Retrieved February 28, 2009 (http://www.fifa.com/classicfootball/history/fifa/historyfifa1.html).

FIFA.com. "Previous FIFA World Cups." Retrieved February 22, 2009 (http://www.fifa.com/worldcup/archive/index.html).

Fiore, Fernando. *The World Cup: The Ultimate Guide to the Greatest Sports Spectacle in the World.* New York, NY: HarperCollins Publishers, 2006.

Hunt, Chris. *The Complete Book of Soccer.* Buffalo, NY: Firefly Books, 2006.

Lisi, Clemente Angelo. *A History of the World Cup: 1930–2006.* Lanham, MD: Scarecrow Press, Inc., 2007.

Miers, Charles, and Elio Trifari, eds. *Soccer! The Game and the World Cup.* New York, NY: Rizzoli International Publications, 1994.

Olbermann, Keith. "Countdown with Keith Olbermann for June 19." June 20, 2006. Retrieved March 6, 2009 (http://www.msnbc.msn.com/id/13438740).

Oliver, Michael. "Lucient Laurent and the Eternal Goal." PitchInvasion.net, June 22, 2008. Retrieved February 22, 2009 (http://pitchinvasion.net/blog/2008/06/22/lucient-laurent-and-the-eternal-goal).

Radnedge, Keir. *The Complete Encyclopedia of Soccer.* London, England: Carlton Books, 2000.

Radnedge, Keir. "Onwards and Upwards?" SI.com, August 20, 2007. Retrieved February 22, 2009 (http://vault.sportsillustrated.cnn.com/vault/article/web/COM1064401/index.htm).

Reuters. "Maradona Proclaims Messi as His Successor." ChinaDaily.com, February 25, 2006. Retrieved February 28, 2009 (http://www.chinadaily.com.cn/english/doc/2006-02/25/content_523966.htm).

Seddon, Peter. *The World Cup's Strangest Moments*. London, England: Robson Books, 2005.

Sher, Misha. "World Cup 2010 Setting a Record." 90soccer.com. Retrieved March 6, 2009 (http://www.90soccer.com/cgi-bin/datacgi/database.cgi?file=v90s&report=sa&ar=253).

Urquhart, Craig. "2010 World Cup: Point of No Return." SouthAfrica.info, February 23, 2009. Retrieved February 28, 2009 (http://www.southafrica.info/2010/project2010column41.htm).

Weiland, Matt, and Sean Wilsey, eds. *The Thinking Fan's Guide to the World Cup*. New York, NY: HarperCollins Publishers, 2006.

Zwane, Simangaliso. "Nelson Mandela—SA's 2010 Envoy." South Africa 2010, July 18, 2008. Retrieved March 6, 2009 (http://www.sa2010.gov.za/node/1020).

ABOUT THE AUTHOR

Diane Bailey was living just down the street when the 1994 World Cup final was played in Pasadena, California. As a growing fan of soccer, she can't wait for the World Cup to come back to the United States. She lives in Kansas and writes on a variety of nonfiction topics.

PHOTO CREDITS